An o

ECO LONDON

Written by
EMMY WATTS

The Culpeper (no.8)

INFORMATION IS DEAD.
LONG LIVE OPINION.

If all information is online, surely books are pointless, right? Especially this one which is printed on paper. Bad, very bad.

Well, the point of this book is not to claim perfection. The point of this book is for all of us to do a bit better. We aren't going to give up on making books and you aren't going to give up on going into town. This book is our highly opinionated guide to what we believe are the most exciting, positive places in London that are reducing their impact so you can too. And here at Hoxton Mini Press we offset all the production costs of our books. We all have a footprint, but let's tread more lightly if we can.

We also have other opinionated guides to:

East London   *London Pubs*

London Architecture   *Sweet London*

Vegan London   *Kids' London*

London Green Spaces   *Escape London*

Independent London

This page: Re:Store (no.10)
Opposite: Petersham Nurseries (no.43)

Petersham Nurseries (no. 43)

LONDONERS CAN BE (ECO-)FRIENDLY.

It's hard not to feel overwhelmed in the face of global climate apocalypse. First of all, let's get over the idea that to be sustainable we have to grow all our own food, never buy anything again and sit at home with the lights off. None of us can exist in a perfectly sustainable way – not you, not me, not a single one of the 56 places in this book. Perfection is deeply impractical. However, that doesn't mean we shouldn't try to do better. By making more informed choices in our daily lives (however small) and being more mindful of our personal impact on the environment (probably bigger than we think), we can all make a real and significant difference – and still have some serious fun while we're at it. This book is a celebration of the small, joyful steps we can all take on the long journey towards sustainability, beginning on our own doorstep.

London is packed with brilliant organisations and small businesses with sustainability at their core, meaning it's never been easier to live more ethically in this city (and we mean really live because, let's face it, we don't put up with the air pollution for nothing). While this is far from an exhaustive list of London locations that are creating less waste, offsetting their emissions or sourcing their produce locally, these ventures are the ones to really get behind – not just because they're making a difference to our little corner of the planet, but because they're doing it in exceptionally creative, stylish and inspiring ways.

Take, for example, cult favourite One Scoop Store (no.54) and its outrageously covetable edit of preloved garments, each one hand-selected by owner Holly Watkins to relieve you of the tedious trawl through the charity-shop rails. Or the brilliant Library of Things (no.51), a London-wide equipment archive offering every occasional-use item you've ever needed but had no desire to stash under the sink. And then there's the delectable DabbaDrop (no.23), a zero-waste Indian takeaway subscription that comes in a reusable tin you can hand back to your rider the following week. All forehead-slappingly simple concepts with the potential to have a real impact on our lives – and on the future of the Earth.

Visiting each of the wonderful (and often magnificently weird) locations in this book and meeting many of the inspiring souls that helped bring them to life has filled me with a genuine sense of optimism. There are so many great things happening in this city; so many amazing people putting everything they've got into fighting for a better world. I really hope that reading it imparts a similar feeling of hope, and that by the time you've finished you feel at least vaguely encouraged, if not empowered, by the idea of what life as a sustainable Londoner might look like – whether that means spending some time with nature in a community-run garden or polishing off a bottle of biodynamic wine.

Emmy Watts
London, June 2022

BEST FOR...

Eco-friendly fashion

Fast fashion is dead! Long live sustainable style! Head to Reformation (no.35) for water-saving denim, before popping into Flax (no.34) for low-impact menswear. Looking for something unique? One Scoop Store (no.54) is the place for curated selections of preloved pieces, while Magpie's (no.53) vintage treasures date back to the 1920s.

Low-impact groceries

Why endure another soulless supermarket when you can get exactly what you need – without so much as a scrap of plastic – at your friendly neighbourhood refill store? Re:Store (no.10), BYGRAM (no.37) and Natoora (no.41) are the best spots to bulk buy in the capital, so load your tote up with jam jars and get replenishing.

Dining out with a difference

Whatever the occasion, London has an eco-friendly feast to suit. Hot date? Try Silo (no.13) for sustainable small plates. Dinner out with the kids? Opt for planet- (and people-) pleasing pizza at Flat Earth (no.9). Or, for really special occasions, book Petersham Nurseries (no.43) (awarded a Green Michelin Star for their sustainably tempting food).

Conscientious cafés

In need a wake-up call? Kiss the Hippo (no.38) and Origin's (no.17) delicious carbon-neutral coffee should do the trick. Or, if it's a lazy brunch you're after, MOTHER's (no.12) vegan comfort food or e5 Bakehouse's (no.11) homegrown daily specials will set you up nicely.

Thoughtful gifts

London's truly great independent stores and stalls make it easy to show someone how much you care about them – and the planet. Head to Wild at Heart (no.42) for naturally abundant blooms in biodegradable wrapping, Borough Wines (no.32) for responsibly-sourced wines they can refill when they're finished, the South Bank Book Market (no.28) for well-thumbed tomes they can pass on and AIDA (no.14) for sustainably-sourced gifts they'll never want to part with.

Treating yourself

Looking after the planet doesn't have to mean neglecting number one. Boutique salons Bangs (no.21), STILL London (no.20) and Glasshouse (no.22) all offer indulgent beauty treatments that don't cost the Earth, while planet-friendly scent specialist Experimental Perfume Club's (no.1) refillable bottles make smelling great feel even better.

An eco evening out

The Kiln (no.55) and Arcola (no.24) theatres hold the stage when it comes to environmental entertainment, while The Lexi's (no.56) green credentials and eclectic screenings make it the go-to for movie buffs. Fancy a tipple? Sustainable bars Nine Lives (no.30) and Midnight Apothecary (no.31) promise killer cocktails with none of the next-day regret (well, a bit less of it anyway).

Getting back to nature

London might be 40 percent green space, but not all of its parks and gardens were created equal. Biodiversity and beauty converge at OmVed Garden (no.48), Camley Street Natural Park (no.46) and Chelsea Physic Garden (no.45), while Dalston Curve Garden (no.7) and Story Garden (no.47) are both doing amazing things for their local (and global) communities.

1

EXPERIMENTAL PERFUME CLUB

DIY fine-fragrance store with minimal packaging

All hail Covent Garden's only carbon-negative perfume boutique, which is reinventing the scent-selection process with its planet-friendly, DIY approach. Simply let one of the perfumiers know your aromatic addictions and aversions, and within minutes you'll have formulated your own personalised scent (you can return your bottle, either in-person or by post, for a refill when you inevitably run dry). Everything EPC makes is PETA-certified vegan, cruelty-free and hand-blended in their London lab, which means they only produce what they sell. Plus emissions are offset with environmental organisation Ecologi, so you can smell good and do good at the same time.

53 Monmouth Street, WC2H 9DG
Nearest station: Covent Garden
experimentalperfumeclub.com

2

PUNK PASTA

Conscientious carbs with attitude

Shaking up London's casual dining scene with its multicoloured pasta shapes and walls daubed with just-as-colourful environmental graffiti, this Bloomsbury newbie caters to those who like their spaghetti with a touch of rebellion (and a complete lack of egg). All dishes are vegan, with dairy and meat replaced by more sustainable ingredients such as jackfruit, seaweed and even wasabi pea dust. 'Hemp Pesto' – a pasta-based dish recreating the Italian classic with hemp, spinach, kale and roasted pine nuts – is a thing of beauty. Pair it with 'Cannelini Bean Bruschetta', a sharable stack of rustic focaccia topped with tasty tomato salsa and lemon oil, and something fiery from the 'Punktails' menu – or even a glass of vegan Spumante from their sustainable wine list.

4 Brunswick Centre, WC1N 1AE
Nearest station: Russell Square
punkpasta.co.uk

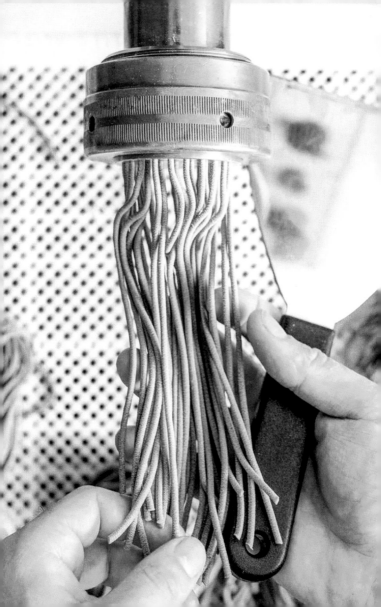

3

L'ESTRANGE LONDON

Elegant menswear cut from renewable fabrics

Less is most definitely more at this no-nonsense boutique, where only the most versatile garments are afforded a spot on one of the chic wooden rails. Every item is a timeless must-have that you'll want to wear every day and, thanks to their high-quality durable materials, you actually can – that's kind of the point. The real hero pieces are the ludicrously adaptable '24 Trouser' (as appropriate on Sunday dog walks as at a summer wedding) and the 'Easy Zip Sweatshirt' (made from an organic cotton that uses 91 percent less irrigated water than the conventional kind). Style, sustainability and sheer simplicity – what more could you want? Free repairs? You're in luck: they do those too.

19 Earlham Street, WC2H 9LL
Nearest station: Covent Garden
lestrangelondon.com

4

FINISTERRE

Enduringly stylish outdoor clothing

Originally founded to clothe Cornish surfers, Finisterre's passion for the sea is matched only by its passion for sustainability – and the brand (whose name means 'end of the Earth' in Latin) has managed to keep this ethos while expanding into casualwear that even landlocked Londoners lust over, alongside more serious outdoor attire. Every item is designed with an environmental emphasis (think organic-only cotton and natural rubber wetsuits), and both unloved and overly-loved garments can be upcycled or fully recycled online in return for money off new treasures. So, you really can wear them to the ends of the Earth.

7 Earlham Street, WC2H 9LL
Nearest station: Covent Garden
finisterre.com

5

HOUSE OF HACKNEY

Maximalist interiors, minimal waste

Regardless of whether you're partial to a bit of William Morris or wouldn't be seen dead investing in floral wallpaper, a visit to House of Hackney's sumptuous showroom is a must. We use the term 'showroom' loosely; the vibe is closer to 'weekend at your eccentric great aunt's townhouse' with its themed rooms and mismatched prints (which might sound oppressive, but trust us, it's great). The going-to-extremes doesn't end with the aesthetics either: this is one of the most sustainable businesses out there with its FSC-certified paper, chemical-free upholstery, low-waste ethos and carbon-neutral status (which they're projected to upgrade to carbon negative by the end of 2022). In fact, it's even B-Corp certified – which means they meet one of the highest international standards of social and environmental responsibility. So, when are we moving in?

St Michael's, Mark Street, EC2A 4ER
Nearest station: Old Street
houseofhackney.com

6

BARBICAN

Arts giant on a sustainable mission

Despite being constructed in the post-war era of energy inefficiency, London's favourite Brutalist arts centre still manages to be one of its most eco-friendly hangouts thanks to its intensified commitment to sustainability. From biodegradable sandwich wrapping and carbon-neutral coffee in the ever-popular Barbican Kitchen to diverse – and in some cases endangered – plants and wildlife in its verdant conservatory, big-budget exhibitions highlighting ecological innovations and the natural world, plus (ahem) concrete plans to reduce its carbon emissions to net zero by 2027, the Barbican is proving it's anything but brutal.

Silk Street, EC2Y 8DS
Nearest station: Barbican
barbican.org.uk

7

DALSTON CURVE GARDEN

Biodiverse green space on an old railway line

Despite being envisaged as 'Dalston's back garden' – due to the high proportion of flat-dwellers in the area – this glorious green space works much harder than your average backyard. The garden grows its own herbs and vegetables for use in the café's hearty soups and seasonal cakes, with proceeds going back into its education and community programme. But it's not just the humans of E8 who benefit: wildlife-friendly trees, shrubs and flowers have been planted in every available corner – so don't be surprised if you find yourself sharing a table with something feathered or furry.

13 Dalston Lane, E8 3DF
Nearest station: Dalston Junction
dalstongarden.org

8

THE CULPEPER

Hyper-seasonal gastropub with a rooftop garden

This stylish pub is named after renowned 17th-century herbalist Nicholas Culpeper, who once lived around the corner – but don't worry, the food here is decidedly more delicious than medicinal. The simple-yet-wholesome dishes in its cosy first-floor restaurant are entirely made from seasonal, local ingredients (some of which are grown in the roof-top garden using fertiliser made from Culpeper's own kitchen leftovers, which makes them very local indeed). Still, an evening spent in its buzzy ground-floor boozer or on its leafy roof terrace is guaranteed to leave you feeling restored – after all, the cocktails are so curatively sweet and syrupy they might as well be tinctures.

40 Commercial Street, E1 6LP
Nearest station: Aldgate East
theculpeper.com

9

FLAT EARTH PIZZAS

Planet-friendly plant-based pizza

It might sound like it's run by globe-deniers, but this Cambridge Heath newbie is actually exceptionally progressive with its innovative flavour combinations and sustainable practices. Swap passé pepperoni (you'll find no meat here – though you can opt for buffalo mozzarella over the vegan variety if you're so inclined) for a tangy kimchi Fiorentina or tongue-tingling Szechuan cauliflower, or brave the Hackney Hot, starring pickled beetroot and fermented hot salsa (Flat Earth's penchant for pickling means intense flavours and longer-lasting produce). Ingredients are locally sourced – often foraged – and seasonal, and not one crumb of unrefined dough (or anything else, for that matter) goes to landfill: any leftovers are turned into fertiliser for use on local farms.

286–290 Cambridge Heath Road, E2 9DA
Nearest station: Cambridge Heath
flatearthpizzas.com

10

RE:STORE

*Un-preachy zero-waste store
with a neighbourhood feel*

Bulk shops might be the future of grocery shopping, but this one has a 'general store' vibe that is reassuringly quaint. In fact, were it not for the whitewashed walls, hunks of 'shamembert' (that's vegan camembert), and silicone menstrual cups, you could feasibly be in a small Somerset village in the 1950s. In fact, you're in an old printworks in Hackney Downs, clutching a tote full of Tupperware and getting soused on a heady aroma of spices and non-toxic cleaning products. Or maybe you're just high on the knowledge that you're helping to eliminate plastic pollution, one Kilner jar at a time.

*Hackney Downs Studios, 17 Amhurst Terrace, E8 2BT
Nearest station: Rectory Road
restorerefill.co.uk*

11

E5 BAKEHOUSE

Ethical bread (and other good things)

Technically it's in E8, not E5, but that's the only thing that feels vaguely deceitful about this Hackney institution, housed in a trio of lofty railway arches beneath London Fields station. Indeed, transparency is key here and almost everything on sale is created from scratch, from the cakes and loaves made using flour stone-milled on site, to the home-roasted coffee and changing daily menu of wholesome dishes celebrating farm-grown veg. A lazy lunch in the walled back garden is always an afternoon well spent, and you categorically cannot leave without a loaf of that sourdough.

395 Mentmore Terrace, E8 3PH
Nearest station: London Fields
e5bakehouse.com

12

MOTHER

Creative vegan fare in a canal-side café

This Hackney Wick hangout takes 'plant-based' to nutritious new heights, stuffing every item on its tempting, brunch-led menu to the brim with naturally flavoursome, nourishing ingredients. Named as a nod to Mother Earth, the café strives to give back what it takes from the planet by using biodegradable, compostable and recycled packaging, offering discounts for bottle and coffee-cup reuse, and utilising only organic, seasonal ingredients. And you too can help to reduce waste, by hoovering up every delicious morsel on your plate – be it the remains of a zesty Bombay toastie, an extravagant MOTHER burger or a wickedly good peanut butter brownie.

Unit 1 Canalside, Here East, E20 3BS
Nearest station: Hackney Wick
mother.works

13

SILO

Virtuous dining (that actually tastes good)

Despite a passion for transparency that often feels like a bit of an overshare, London's original zero-waste restaurant is still one of the best. Pull up a stool at the kitchen-side bar (both made from recycled materials, as is everything, including the plates) and watch the theatre unfold while the exceptionally attentive waiters fill you in on the details of their on-site brewery, laundry and flour mill (hopefully throwing in the odd joke, to take the edge off the worthiness). The 'All In' tasting menu samples the best from this Michelin-Green-Starred eatery (an award highlighting only the finest in sustainable gastronomy) – a tantalising and mainly plant-based procession of earthy flavours and satisfying textures. The minimal-intervention wine isn't bad either.

Unit 7, The White Building, Queen's Yard, E9 5EN
Nearest station: Hackney Wick
silolondon.com

14

AIDA

*Considerately curated lifestyle
store full of indie brands*

AIDA could easily be just another oh-so-trendy Shoreditch boutique, but between its approachable staff, quirky homeware, laid-back café and the fact that it was named after the founders' nan, it manages to be a whole lot more. Not all its products can call themselves sustainable, but a hefty chunk are flying the flag, from Veja's cult vegan trainers to Nkuku's eco-aware and recycled homeware, as well as PETA-approved, Oeko-Tex-certified (meaning no harmful chemicals have been used at all), super-soft organic-cotton slouchy sweatpants made by Colourful Standard. Come for high-quality tees and bum-flattering jeans you'll love forever – or just an idle browse around their excellent selection of smaller, independent brands.

*133 Shoreditch High Street, E1 6JE
Nearest station: Shoreditch High Street
aidashoreditch.co.uk*

15

69B BOUTIQUE

The last word in sustainable style

When this pint-sized boutique first started kitting out Hackney's style elite with planet-friendly clothing over a decade ago, most people thought that 'sustainable fashion' sounded like an oxymoron. Now, partly thanks to them and other trailblazers, we know better. The shop is small, but its selection is extensive, comprising everything from pastel-hued organic cotton basics to timeless statement pieces and ethical accessories – all scrupulously curated down to the last pair of solar-power-produced socks. But it doesn't stop there: staff are paid a London living wage, the store uses renewable energy and there's not a plastic tag in sight. Let's hear it for 69b.

69b Broadway Market, E8 4PH
Nearest station: London Fields
69bboutique.com

16

WHAT MOTHER MADE

Vintage-inspired, uber-local threads

Mother – AKA Charlotte Denn-Cirrone – has made a lot in the decade since she began selling her designs on market stalls. One thing she hasn't created much of though, is waste. Her whimsical clothing for women and 0–8s is made to order, ensuring that every part of each exquisite roll of fabric is utilised. It's a pleasingly local operation, with garments made in Hackney using fabric sourced from Hackney wholesalers and either shipped out or sold from their Hackney boutiques (although there is now a new Muswell Hill branch – we suppose that's just about allowable).

192 Well Street, E9 6QT
Nearest station: Homerton
Other locations: Stoke Newington, Muswell Hill
whatmothermade.co.uk

what
mother
made.

Handmade in Hackney.

17

ORIGIN COFFEE

B-Corp beans in the heart of Shoreditch

Want a shot of integrity with your coffee? Everything about Origin is environmentally friendly, from its B-Corp certification (bestowed only on companies who meet a rigorous ethical and environmental standard) to the sustainable paper in the loos. Customers get a discount for bringing their own cup and can even help themselves to used coffee grounds for their gardens. But it's not only its eco credentials and rotating roster of lively single-origin coffees that make Origin worth visiting: the clean-edged interiors make for the perfect spot to enjoy your daily grind, away from the daily grind. Grab a stool at the bar and slug an aromatic flat white or ask their knowledgeable baristas to recommend which coffee beans or compostable capsules you'd like to have delivered to your front door.

65 Charlotte Road, EC2A 3PE
Nearest station: Old Street
Other locations:
St Pancras (The British Library), Southwark
origincoffee.co.uk

18

THE FISHERIES

Co-working utopia in London Fields

Forget blue-sky thinking, you can literally cloud watch while you work in this laid-back, verdant co-working space, with its tilting glass roof that floods all three of its floors with glorious natural light (and also, thanks to its solar panels, powers your laptop). In fact, you can forget everything you know (and hate) about the office here. Not only are the opening hours flexible, the décor refreshingly un-corporate and the culture entirely non-toxic, the whole building has been designed with its impact on the planet in mind, from upcycled furniture and fittings to rainwater-powered bathrooms and secure indoor bike storage to encourage an eco-friendly commute. They even offer weekly workers' lunches made from locally-sourced produce – never has networking seemed so appealing.

1 Mentmore Terrace, E8 3PN
Nearest station: London Fields
thefisheries.london

19

RUMBLE

A fitness studio that's more than just looks

It's hard not to feel immediately motivated upon entering this Dalston Square gym with its swanky interiors, impossibly buff personal trainers and ridiculously flattering changing-room mirrors – and if that all sounds a bit narcissistic then, well, it is a gym. But beneath Rumble's brawny exterior is a compassionate core: they proudly call themselves London's first carbon-neutral gym (one tree is planted for every session booked) and there's a ban on single-use plastics (in fact, they aim to be completely plastic free in a few years). Come for all-day HIIT training, spinning and yoga in Europe's first 'humming' studio – designed, rather remarkably, to 'mimic Mother Earth's heartbeat'. Leave with rippling muscles and a clear conscience (and probably a ringing in your ears – it's not called Rumble for nothing).

Labyrinth Tower, Dalston Square, E8 3GP
Nearest station: Dalston Junction
Other location: Primrose Hill
rumble-gym.com

20

STILL LONDON

Hackney's sweetest-smelling beauty salon

This tranquil haven in the middle of Dalston couldn't be more appropriately named: time does indeed seem to stand still while you indulge in their dreamy treatments. Whether your complexion is crying out for a facial or your digits are in dire need of attention, STILL's friendly staff are poised to restore them using only the most natural, cruelty-free products. Treatments are designed to provide lethargic Londoners with a break from the city's pollution, drawing inspiration from both the English and Icelandic countryside with hand-harvested, gloriously scented botanical ingredients guaranteed to transport you to your happy place – no matter how far away that is from Kingsland Road.

450 Kingsland Road, e8 4ae
Nearest station: Dalston Junction
still-london.com

21

BANGS LONDON

Hair and beauty without the waste

Dodge past all the other Hoe Street salons and into this industrial-feel space, whose tiny neon sign is the only thing that stops you from overshooting and missing your appointment altogether. In actual fact, Bangs has a lot to shout about: from a staff roster that reads like a who's-who of London's top beauty therapists to a list of cruelty-free treatments the length of a Chinese takeaway menu. What's more, they partner with hair-and-beauty recycling specialists Handle to recycle all of the salon's waste – right down to the cuttings swept from the exposed concrete floor. If that's not something to shout about, we don't know what is.

66–68 Hoe Street, E17 4PG
Nearest station: Walthamstow Central
bangslondon.com

22

GLASSHOUSE SALON

Transparent hairdressing

They say people who live in glass houses shouldn't throw stones – so it's a good job you'd never catch this salon's friendly staff passing judgement. Yet their laidback attitude belies a rigorous approach to sustainability: all waste is recycled via the innovative Green Salon Collective scheme (who convert colour waste into electricity, preventing it from polluting our water supplies and soil) and Handle (who even use hair waste to stop oil spills), while products are formulated using natural ingredients and absolutely no harsh chemicals. Plus, hairdressers here are fountains of mane-maintenance knowledge, meaning you leave with healthy locks and the tools needed to keep them that way.

139 Mare Street, E8 3RH
Nearest station: London Fields
glasshousesalon.co.uk

23

DABBADROP

Indian takeaway, done right

Fancy a curry? Step away from the gloopy tikka masala, delivered via a CO_2-oozing moped in a single-use box. DabbaDrop is delightfully different, dispensing its naturally healthy, explosively flavoursome plant-based curries by bike or emission-free vehicles in satisfyingly stackable reusable tins (which you can hand back to your rider the following week – or the one after that, depending on whether you choose a weekly or fortnightly subscription). The menu journeys to a different South Asian region each week, so stick around to sample everything from delicate Hyderabadi biryanis to hearty Kashmiri jackfruit keemas. DabbaDrop's pre-ordering policy also means their meals generate minimal food waste – finally, a takeaway that gives back.

Delivers to most of north, east and southeast London.
dabbadrop.co.uk

24

ARCOLA THEATRE

Pioneering performances in the heart of Hackney

Only in Dalston could you find a theatre so lacking in pretension. Located in a former factory just off Kingsland Road, Arcola oozes East End charisma with its bare brick walls, local beers and a very Hackney commitment to championing diversity and busting taboos through its impactful shows – many of them accessible to low earners via a 'pay what you can' scheme. The trailblazing doesn't end with the programming either: energy is generated via on-site solar panels and a carbon-neutral heating system, and the water-saving toilets demand a look even if you don't need to go. Aim for an outdoor performance to enjoy contemporary drama and music in a space with even more atmosphere than Shakespeare's Globe.

24 Ashwin Street, E8 3DL
Nearest station: Dalston Junction
arcolatheatre.com

25

GOOD HOTEL

Riverside rooms that look good and do good

This four-star 'floatel' (that's a floating hotel) takes upcycling to impressive depths, having set up shop in a converted Dutch detention centre currently tethered to the Royal Victoria Docks. But while the décor is minimalist and the bedrooms small, this chic concrete inn feels anything but prisonlike thanks to the panoramic views afforded by its huge windows and rooftop bar. The fact that all profits are reinvested into educational projects might be the hotel's biggest boast (that, and its tempting small-plates-focused menu), but its planet-preservation efforts aren't far behind its philanthropy: they serve ale made from surplus bread and even have London's first Seabin, a 'floating rubbish bin' that syphons litter from the river. If anything, 'Good' feels like a bit of an understatement.

Royal Victoria Dock, Western Gateway, E16 1FA
Nearest station: Royal Victoria
goodhotel.co

26

WAHACA

Eco-friendly enchiladas

Behind the scenes, this street-food chain is squaring up against the climate crisis (it was the first UK restaurant to be certified as carbon neutral back in 2016). On the surface though, it's all fun and frijoles. Cute carbon-impact menu symbols help diners make informed decisions without being preachy, while the fava-bean Wahacamole is as delightfully fresh and creamy as the original without a scrap of water-guzzling avocado. Hell, even the building is fun – the South Bank branch is built from eight brightly coloured recycled shipping containers decked out with playful upcycled furnishings. Heading there for a Sunday brunch? Treat yourself to a spicy Michelada, Mexico's answer to the Bloody Mary.

Queen Elizabeth Hall, Belvedere Road, SE1 8XX
Nearest station: Waterloo
Other locations: multiple, see website
wahaca.co.uk

27

LOWIE

Made-to-last contemporary womenswear

This boutique is sticking two fingers up to fast fashion by selling clothes so joyful you'll never want to take them off. Flattering silhouettes and thoughtful fabrics are a common thread running through every garment (30 percent use upcycled or recycled materials and 50 percent are manufactured with low-impact techniques) but in every other way they're fetchingly unique, with bold prints and inspired details. While Lowie's focus on traditional craftsmanship means its clothes are made to last, free lifetime repairs are available for those you've loved a bit too vigorously, with plans to introduce monthly upcycling workshops for the ones you've literally worn to death.

18 Half Moon Lane, SE24 9HU
Nearest station: Herne Hill
ilovelowie.com

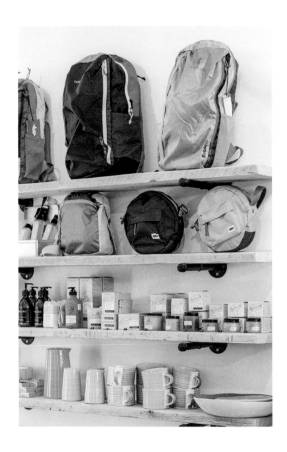

28

SOUTH BANK BOOK MARKET

Preloved books under Waterloo Bridge

With its backdrop of big-name landmarks, few things feel as 'London' as a rummage through this open-air market's myriad tomes – and yet there's something unmistakably Parisian about its romantic riverside location. Old prints, posters and bits of vinyl make the odd appearance on the rows of trestle tables, but second-hand books are very much the star of this show, from classic novels to more recent releases – many in mint condition. Stock moves fast and the thrill of bagging a bargain is all the more gratifying when you know you're saving a preloved paperback from the landfill.

Under Waterloo Bridge, 337–338 Belvedere Road
Nearest station: Waterloo
southbanklondon.com

29

MALLOW

Thoughtfully sourced, wildly delicious vegan fare

This plant-based, low-waste newcomer from the team behind vegan pioneers Mildreds is cleverly named after a flower whose entire form is edible, right down to its roots. The marshmallow references are everywhere, from the sugary pink tiles to the 'Campfire Marshmallow' dessert, but mallow's real strength is in its mouth-watering mains, whose first-rate ingredients are largely sourced from neighbouring Borough Market. Order the Urfa Celeriac Skewer or the Market Thali, or – even better – both.

1 Cathedral Street, SE1 9DE
Nearest station: London Bridge
mallowlondon.com

30

NINE LIVES BAR

*Zero-waste tropical lounge
with a moreish Mexican menu*

Forget the cocktails for a second, this dimly lit Cali-cool basement bar is worth the trip for its sustainable tacos alone. If we had nine lives, we'd spend at least one of them eating nothing but their beer-battered banana blossom baja (impossible to order without lisping). To wash it down? Try the Coco de Mer, an intoxicating mix of blended rums (including one made from banana waste) and salted caramel that's finished with a fat sprig of rosemary from the garden out back, and tastes all the better slurped from an eco-friendly bamboo straw.

*8 Holyrood Street, SE1 2EL
Nearest station: London Bridge
ninelivesbar.com*

31

MIDNIGHT APOTHECARY

Cocktails overlooking an underwater tunnel

Crackling fire pits, subterranean gatherings and botanical concoctions stuffed with homegrown herbs. It may sound like a scene from *The Craft*, but this is just a normal night out in Rotherhithe (in the summer months, at least). These otherworldly experiences begin on the flourishing rooftop that crowns the southside of Brunel's Thames Tunnel – an engineering masterpiece and the first of its kind ever built – with patrons given two hours to savour as many flavour-intense, locally-sourced (even the spirits and beers are made in London), seasonal cocktails as they desire, surrounded by the plants that helped make them. Then it's time to descend the stairs for an entertaining tour of the Tunnel's cavernous entrance shaft with charismatic actor (and local) Tim Thomas. All positively bewitching.

Railway Avenue, SE16 4LF
Nearest station: Rotherhithe
themidnightapothecary.co.uk

32

BOROUGH WINES

Responsible, refillable wines

Hidden among the tantalizing food stalls of London's oldest market, this store's wine-on-tap concept might sound dangerous, but when you consider the number of bottles it saves, it makes a whole barrel of sense. Not all of Borough Wine's offerings come from kegs, but they do all hail from small indie makers and many are vegan, organic, biodynamic or all three. Wines (and beers) are also available by the glass, so you can try them out while you wander the market in search of the perfect cheese to pair them with, before returning for a bottle (or three) to take home.

Borough Market, SE1 1TL
Nearest station: London Bridge
boroughwines.co.uk

33

BLANC

Not just another dry cleaner

Dry cleaning is dry cleaning, right? Wrong. Step into BLANC's white-walled Chelsea boutique and you'll feel more like you're entering a luxury spa than dropping off your washing. Gone are the rows of plastic-wrapped suits and the unmistakable stench of chemicals, replaced by delicate botanical aromas and shelves packed with natural cleaning products. BLANC's non-toxic processes are designed to be much kinder on your skin and the planet than traditional dry cleaning, and clothes emerge looking better than they've ever looked. Who says you shouldn't air your dirty laundry in public?

85 Lower Sloane Street, SW1W 8DA
Nearest station: Sloane Square
Other locations: Marylebone, Notting Hill,
South Kensington
blancliving.co

34

FLAX LONDON

Long-life linen menswear

Linen might be one of the lowest-impact fibres available, but it's also one of the most overlooked: snubbed for its short-lived seasonality and tendency to wrinkle. Determined to prove that linen is for life, not just for summer, this smart menswear brand offers everything from lightweight shirts to perennial workwear jackets and heavier options for winter. Garments are made to last (traditional manufacturing techniques and classic shapes ensure their durability), but still pack plenty of fun thanks to a vibrant choice of colours and virtually endless layerability. You'll probably still have to get the iron out though – sorry about that.

101 Golborne Road, W10 5NL
Nearest station: Westbourne Park
flaxlondon.com

35
REFORMATION

Hip yet heartfelt womenswear boutique

While this LA brand acknowledges that being naked is 'the number one most sustainable option', they've accepted that public nudity is frowned upon and come up with the next-best thing. Reformation began life as a vintage store and still offers a killer selection of preloved treasures alongside their own label, which includes covetable jeans made from water-saving denim, recycled-cashmere knitwear and even sustainable wedding dresses. But the best bit has to be the fitting rooms, where you can change the lighting, select your own music and order different sizes to be delivered straight to your cubicle – even more reason to stay naked a little longer.

186 Westbourne Grove, W11 2RH
Nearest station: Notting Hill Gate
Other location: Shoreditch
thereformation.com

36

GOLDFINGER DESIGN

More than a furniture store

Named for the Modernist architect and not the Bond villain (although, rumour has it Fleming named his infamous antagonist after said Modernist architect), this award-winning social enterprise has thankfully committed itself to doing good rather than evil. Based at the foot of Goldfinger's iconic Trellick Tower, the chic homeware store and adjoining workshop makes and sells bespoke furniture, with all profits going back into charitable initiatives. Every object is crafted with its ecological impact in mind, from non-toxic candles to knives carved from the workshop's own offcuts – over 400 tonnes of material have been rescued from landfills and transformed into heirloom-worthy homeware. Goldfinger also offers woodwork and craft courses, equipping the next generation with all the tools they need to continue the good work.

13-15 Golborne Road, W10 5NY
Nearest station: Westbourne Park
goldfinger.design

37

BYGRAM

Bulk buying at its best

Thought all zero-waste stores were made equal? This Fulham Road spot sets itself apart from the rest, luring you in with its white-tiled floors and lush greenery, convincing you to buy three times as much as you came in for (even if that's not really the point), and leaving you in no doubt that this is the way forward when it comes to grocery shopping. New products are added every month and the wall of detergent refills is one of the best we've seen (and by now, we've seen quite a few). So, get down to sw6 and fill your boots – or y'know, some Tupperware.

795 Fulham Road, sw6 5HD
Nearest station: Parsons Green
bygram.co.uk

38

KISS THE HIPPO

Carbon-negative coffee shop

It's almost impossible to stand out in the capital's ridiculously oversaturated coffee-shop scene, especially when you're tucked away on a backstreet in Fitzrovia, but this bright, wood-panelled spot manages it – and not just because it has a silly name and a cool logo. Kiss the Hippo's coffee is exceptionally good and tastes all the better for knowing exactly where it came from (via farmers paid at least twice the Fair-Trade price, and the world's most environmentally friendly coffee roaster, which uses 80 percent less fuel than a traditional one). Add to that their completely compostable cups and used coffee grounds that get turned into biofuel, and you know they truly are brewing something good.

51 Margaret Street, W1W 8SG
Nearest station: Oxford Circus
Other locations: Chelsea, Richmond, King's Cross
kissthehippo.com

39

MERCATO MAYFAIR

Sustainable food market on former holy ground

An eco-friendly eatery inside an erstwhile Mayfair church might sound stuffy, but there's no need to iron your Sunday best. Granted, Mercato's Grade I-listed neoclassical backdrop is as grand as they come, but the two-storey food market that calls it home is reassuringly informal – and the food is sinfully good. Fluffy bao buns, velvety gelato, buttery pasta and wickedly strong cocktails are just a handful of the unearthly delights you can sample here, and they're all made from locally sourced, sustainable ingredients. Single-use plastic is obviously a sacrilege (and banned on site), but well-behaved dogs are welcome.

St Mark's, North Audley Street, W1K 6ZA
Nearest station: Bond Street
Other locations: Elephant and Castle, Canary Wharf
mercatometropolitano.com

40

FALLOW

Modern Mayfair restaurant with zero-waste ethos

This hip dining spot is all about creating moreish dishes from the ingredients that other restaurants overlook – be it bone-marrow-fortified brioche, burger sauce magicked from surplus cucumbers or a whole cod's head confidently plated up as a main. Sharing is encouraged as much as wastefulness is not, with dishes designed to be communal (though you might have something to say about that if you've ordered the decadent kombu corn ribs). And there are kitchen-side seats offering insight into the chefs' craft – just in case you want to steal some creative ideas for your weeknight dinners.

2 St James's Market, SW1Y 4RP
Nearest station: Piccadilly Circus
fallowrestaurant.com

41

NATOORA

Not your average greengrocer

Anyone who's ever doubted the sex appeal of fruit and vegetables should immediately head to this Fulham Road fresh-produce store and check out the juicy specimens on offer. Inside a concrete-walled boutique, bouquets of meaty artichokes sit pretty in ceramic vases, while glossy bell peppers and fat radishes spill seductively from grey shelves. Their allure is largely down to Natoora's rejection of perennial availability in favour of 'radical seasonality' (a concept that trickles into its tantalising café menu) and an emphasis on the grower, with details of origin next to each variety. The whole store is plastic-free, too – well, naturally.

309 Fulham Road, SW10 9QH
Nearest station: South Kensington
Other locations: Sloane Square, Portobello, Chiswick,
Bermondsey (Saturdays only)
natoora.co.uk

42

WILD AT HEART

Naturally beautiful eco-friendly blooms

A public toilet on a traffic island in Notting Hill doesn't sound like an obvious place to pick up a hand-tied bouquet of pink peonies, but there are nothing but sweet aromas emanating from this compact florist. Always careful not to overstock their responsibly-sourced and seasonal blooms to ensure little to no flower waste (although if they do run out of your favourite, their expert florists will be happy to rustle up something out-of-the-ordinary), they also have plans to switch to electric delivery vehicles only. The result is flowers that look freshly plucked from an English garden, not from a petrol station forecourt.

Turquoise Island, 222 Westbourne Grove, W11 2RH
Nearest station: Notting Hill Gate
wildatheart.com

43

PETERSHAM NURSERIES CAFÉ

*Classy greenhouse dining
in a plant-filled wonderland*

The name makes it sound lowkey, but this riverside favourite is actually a Michelin-Starred restaurant (and not just any Michelin Star, but a Green Michelin Star). Still, it's pretty laid-back: floors are bare, tables are cloth-less, food is simple (in a really good way) and the staff are warm and unpretentious. It's expensive, sure, but not flashy. There's no need for flashiness when you've got the most magical garden in London right outside – full of edible plants that will no doubt appear on your plate. Pick up a cutting from the adjacent nursery and take a bit of that abundant beauty home with you.

Off Church Lane, Petersham Road, TW10 7AB
Nearest station: Richmond
Other location: Covent Garden
petershamnurseries.com

44

APRICITY

Feel-good food that does good too

Few words would do justice to the magic of this Mayfair newcomer, and yet its name – an archaic word meaning 'the warmth of the sun in winter' – succeeds splendidly. The latest venture from Chantelle Nicholson (whose previous venture was awarded a Green Michelin Star), Apricity serves up happiness on a plate – proving that eating sustainably is as good for the soul as it is the planet. Elegant staff in low-impact uniforms not only know everything about the food they serve, but are rightfully proud of it: 'wasted' dip is whipped up from the kitchen's excess veg; wild fish is caught from British waters and lettuce is grown at a hydroponic farm down the road (and that's just the starters).

68 Duke Street, W1K 6JU
Nearest station: Bond Street
apricityrestaurant.com

45

CHELSEA PHYSIC GARDEN

Botanical archive on the banks of the Thames

Its imposing façade makes a trip to London's oldest botanic garden feel more like an illicit foray onto private land than a visit to the recipient of a Green Tourism award. However, once you've paid the fee (the plants don't look after themselves, y'know) and entered this 400-year-old 'living library', you'll see why they're so cagey. This magical space is home to 5,000 species, including some of the most endangered plants on the planet, and its team knows a thing or two about protecting them (like how its high walls create a plant-protecting 'heat trap'). Stick around and you could learn a hell of a lot. Just don't get locked in.

66 Royal Hospital Road, SW3 4HS
Nearest station: Sloane Square
chelseaphysicgarden.co.uk

46

CAMLEY STREET NATURAL PARK

Innovative urban wildlife sanctuary

This picturesque nature reserve in the heart of busy King's Cross is run by the London Wildlife Trust on the site of a former coal-storage depot. Today it offers two acres of vital green space, not just to the diverse wildlife and pioneering environmental studies it hosts, but to local humans in search of a little inner-city calm. As you spot nesting coots from the floating canal platform – a cup of the on-site café's exceptional coffee in one hand and one of its doorstop bagels in the other – you'll need little convincing that all urban parks should be this wild. Combine your visit with a (potentially pricey) mooch around Coal Drops Yard's spectacular shopping complex – a short but scenic walk away across the Somers Town Bridge.

12 Camley Street, King's Cross, N1C 4PW
Nearest station: King's Cross St Pancras
wildlondon.org.uk/camley-street-natural-park

47

STORY GARDEN

A green space that nurtures community

This bountiful urban garden might be tucked behind the British Library, but that's not how it got its moniker. Managed by an educational charity, the Story Garden was actually named as a tribute to the countless locals and visitors who frequent it, and their diverse characters and backgrounds. While everything that happens here is centred on the community – whether that's residents growing their own food, sustainable cookery classes for young people, or harvesting vegetables to donate to food banks – you don't need to be local to enjoy it. Eco-enthusiasts from far and wide are more than welcome to pop down with a picnic and soak up the calm vibes and endless gardening inspiration.

Ossulston Street, NW1 1DF
Nearest station: King's Cross St Pancras
globalgeneration.co.uk

48

OMVED GARDEN

Secret garden on a not-so-secret mission

This north London garden's owners want to talk to us. Don't worry, it's nothing serious – they just want a quick chat about food, climate change and the future of the planet. Alright, so it is serious, but what if this 'chat' could take the form of a supper club, with dishes made from low-impact, organic home-grown crops; or a preserving workshop designed to transform the way you think about food waste; or even an evening of storytelling focused around local nature – all immersed in the uncommonly beautiful surroundings of an ecologically diverse three-acre secret hillside garden, with breath-taking views over Highgate Woods? Okay, we're listening.

Townsend Yard, N6 5JF
Nearest station: Highgate
omvedgardens.com

49

GROWING COMMUNITIES

Ethical farmers' market

Seen one farmers' market, seen 'em all? This west Hackney institution might change your mind with its remarkable community spirit and unwavering commitment to organic and bio-dynamic farming (it's the only UK farmers' market where traders must be certified as one of the two). The veg may be some of the most flavourful (and reassuringly seasonal) we've ever had but there's plenty more to sample and stock up on, from zesty ferments to choice meats sourced from animals reared to the highest welfare standards. Any questions? Ask the farmers themselves – most of whom hail from within 60 miles of London.

St Paul's Church,
182 Stoke Newington Rd, N16 7UE
Nearest station: Rectory Road
growingcommunities.org

50

SNIFFLES

Spa and shop for conscientious canines

Even pampered pooches can do their bit to save the planet thanks to this Heath-side hound hub in Hampstead (try saying that three times fast). Sniffles is a sustainability-focused grooming salon, doggy day-care centre and pet store all in one. Aside from its own-brand organic dog shampoos and conditioners – which are used during the grooming process – it stocks an impressive variety of eco-friendly products for responsible pup parents, from refillable natural treat tins to bamboo food bowls, compostable poop bags and colourful toys made entirely from recycled plastic. Day-care dogs also get a daily walk on the Heath – one of the most biodiverse green spaces in the capital.

6 Fleet Road, NW3 2QS
Nearest station: Gospel Oak
sniffles-spa.co.uk

51

LIBRARY OF THINGS

Community equipment rental

If this social business gets its way there will be a Library of Things, as well as one of their affordable repair shops (so the equipment you do own will last a lot longer), in every neighbourhood that wants one – and who doesn't love the idea of being able to rent a power drill (or a Playstation, or a projector, or a pasta maker, or a tent, or a heavy-duty pressure washer) at a moment's notice? 'Things' are hireable from any of their eight locations across London on a daily or weekly basis for a fraction of their retail price and are simply returned to their locker when you're done, helping to save money and the planet by drastically reducing wasteful, one-time purchases – as well as, crucially for Londoners, saving storage space.

Kentish Town Library,
262–266 Kentish Town Road, NW5 2AA
Nearest station: Kentish Town
Other locations: multiple, see website
libraryofthings.co.uk

52

HALF CUT MARKET

Experimental off-licence with eco focus

Is it a corner shop? Is it a wine bar? More of a deli, perhaps? Oh, and look, there's loads of indie beer. This Camden newbie may not have made up its mind what it is yet, but that's all part of the fun. Its owners – four friends united by a love of good booze – buzz with enthusiasm, whether they're pouring you a glass of minimal-intervention wine or ringing up a jar of ethically sourced sardines. Half Cut also offers a packed programme of tastings, workshops and supper clubs, and there's even talk of an in-store plastic and cork drop-off centre. Phew, this place doesn't do things by halves.

396 York Way, N7 9LW
Nearest station: Caledonian Road
halfcut.world

53

MAGPIE VINTAGE

A treasure trove of preloved and upcycled clothes

Magpies might call to mind ill-fortune, but you'd struggle to visit this Camden Passage boutique and not get lucky. Owner Alice Lockspeiser is an expert in tracking down only the most exceptional of preloved garments, from elegant 1930s gowns to frilly 1980s jumpsuits. And they also offer upcycled pieces, hand-stitched by the team in north London, so you can pick up an on-trend crochet cardigan or a dress crafted from hand-embroidered tablecloths. Plus, free repairs come as standard, they plant a tree for every £40 spent, fabric scraps are turned into minimal-waste accessories and all packaging is plastic-free – all the more reason to leave your superstitions at the door.

3 Camden Passage, N1 8EA
Nearest station: Angel
Other location (vintage stall): Brick Lane Vintage Market
magpievintageclothing.com

54

ONE SCOOP STORE

Cult clothing that doesn't cost the Earth

You're almost guaranteed to find threads you want to wear forever at this cool Stokey boutique, so exceptional is the curation of their preloved pieces. And if you do, be sure to snap them up – new stock often sells out in seconds via their Instagram. While One Scoop's forte is edgy second-hand statement wear, the selection is always eclectic, comprising everything from ball gowns unearthed at thrift markets to designer pool sliders sourced from private sellers. And there's an impressive number of cult labels in the mix, too – think Meadows, Mother of Pearl, Ganni, Shrimps and more. Prices are largely a fraction of the original value and yet everything feels fresh and contemporary, which begs the question – why buy new?

101 Stoke Newington High Street, N16 0PH
Nearest station: Stoke Newington
onescoopstore.com

55

KILN THEATRE

Playhouse that puts its community centre stage

It makes sense that a theatre famed for original plays highlighting human rights issues would also give a damn about the planet – and the people who occupy its own little corner of it. This well-loved playhouse and cinema might be big, but it radiates neighbourhood energy, with productions chosen to reflect the cultural diversity of the area, a buzzy café that spills out onto Kilburn High Road and a communal prop store that other theatres can raid. Sets are inventive and continually recycled – which is something of a theme at Kiln, whose sustainable practices range from converting all the kitchen's cooking oil into biofuel (via food-waste-specialists Olleco) to inviting locals to drop off unwanted electrical items for recycling. Because even microwaves deserve an encore.

269 Kilburn High Road, NW6 7JR
Nearest station: Brondesbury
kilntheatre.com

56

THE LEXI CINEMA

A big screen with an even bigger heart

There are few activities so escapist as a night at the cinema, and with its eco-friendly building and social-enterprise status, this Kensal Rise gem is really upping the feel-good factor. Supposing you demand more from your local picture house than knowing that all profits get sent to a pioneering sustainability institute in rural South Africa, you can also expect an eclectic assortment of films, a fully stocked bar and volunteers who know their Lynch from their Fincher. Be sure to grab a (reusable) bucket of freshly popped popcorn or a glass jar (also reusable) of pick and mix before the show starts – it's well worth missing the trailers for.

INDEX

69b Boutique, *15*

AIDA, *14*

Apricity, *44*

Arcola Theatre, *24*

Bangs London, *21*

Barbican, *6*

BLANC, *33*

Borough Wines, *32*

BYGRAM, *37*

Camley Street Natural Park, *46*

Chelsea Physic Garden, *45*

DabbaDrop, *23*

Dalston Curve Garden, *7*

e5 Bakehouse, *11*

Experimental Perfume Club, *1*

Fallow, *40*

Finisterre, *4*

Flat Earth Pizzas, *9*

Flax London, *34*

Glasshouse Salon, *22*

Goldfinger Design, *36*

Good Hotel, *25*

Growing Communities, *49*

Half Cut Market, *52*

House of Hackney, *5*

Kiln Theatre, *55*

Kiss the Hippo, *38*

L'Estrange London, *3*

Library of Things, *51*

Lowie, *27*

Magpie Vintage, *53*

mallow, *29*

Mercato Mayfair, *39*

Midnight Apothecary, *31*

MOTHER, *12*

Natoora, *41*

Nine Lives Bar, *30*

OmVed Garden, *48*

One Scoop Store, *54*

Origin Coffee, *17*

Petersham Nurseries Café, *43*

Punk Pasta, *2*

Re:Store, *10*

Reformation, *35*

RUMBLE, *19*

Silo, *13*

Sniffles, *50*

South Bank Book Market, *28*

STILL London, *20*

Story Garden, *47*

The Culpeper, *8*

The Fisheries, *18*

The Lexi Cinema, *56*

Wahaca, *26*

What Mother Made, *16*

Wild at Heart, *42*

IMAGE CREDITS

69b Boutique © Charlotte Schreiber; AIDA © Chris Snook / AIDA / Studio Wilhelm; Apricity (all images) © Stefan Jansen Birch; Arcola Theatre © Charlotte Schreiber; Bangs © Charlotte Schreiber; Barbican © Nathaniel Noir / Alamy Stock Photo; BLANC © BLANC; Borough Wines © Steve Hawkins / Alamy Stock Photo; BYGRAM © Larry Jordan; Camley Street Natural Park (first image) © Martin Usborne; Camley Street Natural Park (double-page spread) © Henrietta Williams; Chelsea Physic Garden © Sam Bush; The Culpeper (intro p.2) © Veerle Evans; The Culpeper (all images) © Veerle Evans; DabbaDrop (all images) © Brendan McGinty; Dalston Curve Garden (first image) © Charlotte Schreiber; Dalston Curve Garden (double-page spread) © Martin Usborne; e5 Bakehouse (all images) © Helen Cathcart; Experimental Perfume Club © Experimental Perfume Club; Fallow (first page) © Lisa Tse; Fallow (second page) © Steven Joyce; Fallow (third page) © Dominic Rowntree (@samphire-andsalsify); Finisterre © Charlotte Schreiber; The Fisheries © Fisheries London Ltd; Flat Earth Pizzas © Aleksandra Boruch / Flat Earth Pizzas; Flax London © Flax London Ltd; Glasshouse Salon © Genevieve Lutkin; Goldfinger Design © Ben Peter Catchpole; Good Hotel (first and second image) © Good Hotel, Royal Victoria Dock; Good Hotel (third image) © Anne Travel Foodie; Growing Communities © Sara Kiyo Popowa; Half Cut Market © Caitlin Isola; House of Hackney (all images) © House of Hackney / Emma Harries; Kiln Theatre © Charlotte Schreiber; Kiss the Hippo © Kiss the Hippo Coffee Ltd; L'Estrange London © L'Estrange London / Sarah Bates; The Lexi Cinema © Zute Lightfoot; Library of Things © Library of Things; Lowie © Charlotte Schreiber; Magpie Vintage © Collette Fawcett / Saffron Beal; mallow (all images) © mallow; Mercato Mayfair © Mercato Metropolitano; Midnight Apothecary © Charlotte Schreiber; MOTHER (first image) © Sam A Harris; MOTHER (second image) © Jaak London; Natoora © James Bedford; Nine Lives Bar © Steven Tran (@tranvfood); OmVed Gardens (all images) © Thomas Broadhead; One Scoop Store © Charlotte Schreiber; Origin Coffee © Gary Handley; Petersham Nurseries Café (intro p.4, p.6-7) © Andrew Montgomery; Petersham Nurseries Café (all images) © Andrew Montgomery; Punk Pasta (first image) © Charlotte Schreiber; Punk Pasta (second and third image) © Richard Jarrett; Re:Store (intro p.5) © Charlotte Schreiber; Re:Store (all images) © Charlotte Schreiber; Reformation © Charlotte Schreiber; RUMBLE © Charlotte Schreiber; Silo London (first page) © Sam A Harris / Silo; Silo London (double-page spread) © Matt Russell / Silo; Sniffles © Charlotte Schreiber; South Bank Book Market © Monica Wells / Alamy Stock Photo; Still London © Charlotte Schreiber; Story Garden © Charlotte Schreiber; Wahaca © Charlotte Nott-Macaire; What Mother Made © Sarah Lincoln; Wild at Heart © Rachael Smith.

CONTRIBUTORS

Emmy Watts is a Yorkshire-born writer specialising in fun things to do in London with kids. She lives in Camden with her own two children, who she's attempting to raise as sustainably as possible (though that's easier said than done given their shared aversion to vegetables and penchant for pink plastic).

Hoxton Mini Press is a small indie publisher based in east London. We make books about London (and beyond) with a dedication to lovely, sustainable production and brilliant photography. When we started the company, people told us 'print was dead'; we wanted to prove them wrong. Books are no longer about information but objects in their own right: things to collect and own and inspire. We are an environmentally conscious publisher, committed to offsetting our carbon footprint. This book, for instance, is 100 percent carbon compensated, with offset purchased from Stand for Trees.

Eco London: An Opinionated Guide
First edition

Published in 2022 by Hoxton Mini Press, London
Copyright © Hoxton Mini Press 2022. All rights reserved.

Text by Emmy Watts
Copy-editing by Florence Filose and Octavia Stocker
Design by Richard Mason
Production by Sarah-Louise Deazley

With thanks to Matthew Young for initial series design

Please note: we recommend checking the websites listed for each
entry before you visit for the latest information on price, opening times
and pre-booking requirements.

A CIP catalogue record for this book is available from the British Library.

ISBN: 978-1-914314-20-9

Printed and bound by OZGraf, Poland

Hoxton Mini Press is an environmentally conscious publisher, committed
to offsetting our carbon footprint. This book is 100 percent carbon compensated,
with offset purchased from Stand For Trees.

For every book you buy from our website, we plant a tree:
www.hoxtonminipress.com